How to Be Born Again

Other Poetry Titles from Quarry Press

How to Be Born Again

COLIN MORTON

To Pat
at Penny University
Colin Morton
4/92

QUARRY PRESS

Some of these poems, many in earlier versions, were published in *Anthology of Magazine Verse, Anthos, Arc, Bywords, Canadian Literature, Capital Poets, Fiddlehead, Grain, New Federation, Opus, Orbis, Poetry Canada Review, Prairie Fire, Printed Matter, Prospice, Quarry, When Is a Poem?* and *Zymergy.* Italicized passages in "Letters from Kentucky" are excerpted from the published letters of John Keats.

For support and encouragement, the author thanks the members of First Draft. Special thanks for valuable comments and advice to Susan McMaster and Nadine McInnis. "A Bouquet for Blaine" is for Blaine Marchand. Financial assistance from the Ontario Arts Council and the Regional Municipality of Ottawa-Carleton is appreciated.

The publisher acknowledges the financial assistance of The Canada Council and the Ontario Arts Council.

Canadian Cataloguing in Publication Data

Morton, Colin, 1948 —
  How to Be Born Again

Poems,
ISBN 1-55082-036-2

  I. Title.

PS8576.0746H69 1992 C811.54 C92-090056-9
PR9199.3.M67H69 1992

Cover art entitled "Senecio" by Paul Klee, reproduced by permission of Kunstermuseum, Basel, Switzerland.

Design by Keith Abraham. Typesetting by Susan Hannah. Printed and bound in Canada by Hignell Printing, Winnipeg, Manitoba.

Published by Quarry Press, Inc.,
P.O. Box 1061, Kingston, Ontario K7L 4Y5.

For Mary Lee and Jeffrey

Contents

The History of the Future Tense

Famous
Lovers

How to Be Born Again

We can never be born enough
      e.e. cummings

After many years of marriage we can arrive at the same house,
eat meals and wash dishes together, kiss and go to sleep in the
same bed, hardly looking at one another. Yet sometimes, we are
so much in love we disconnect the telephone and don't go out all
day; we don't even pick up the mail when it drops through the
slot in the door.

Then, grown weary of this life, you lie on your side and
say to me, Let's be born all over again. Let's be born our
parents' age and meet in London during the blitz and lock
ourselves in a hotel room, refusing to hide in the shelter when
the sirens blow because we would rather die in each others' arms
than go back alone to our hospitals and airfields. Let's not leave
that room even when the whisky runs out.

I reply, Let's be born in the last century and make love
through Victoria's jubilee. Let's be disowned by your father the
Czar and betray the Revolution in order to run away on the
Titanic. Let's melt icebergs with our kisses and cruise past the
Statue of Liberty without fanfare, a miracle no one notices.

Let's be born in Troy, such lovers that no one pays any
attention to Helen, no warships are launched, Hector's life is
spared, Rome is never built, and history ends in a blaze of
passion before it gets started.

Let's be born in a spaceship near the speed of light and
never die.

Beginning

1

Circle and bow to the wick
circle and bow
the small dance
of an ash in the candle

wheel and reel
waves dance
round a stone
half submerged

(in the beginning simple instances will serve)

the spring round which a settlement grows

one word   endlessly
bears the rise and fall of voices

an island   a peak
a point defining the space around.

1

In the valley
circled by the sun
there is nothing outside the valley

we are the center
one woman
one man
one tree
two dimensions stretched between
two directions

a circular definition.

2

But the sun does not
roll round our horizon
there are further fields that ripen
reaper or no

a stranger comes down from the hillside
with tales of a valley beyond

this frame is exposed

look
the tree is fallen
the woman is leaving with the stranger.

1

There is no water in the wave
the wave is in the water

there is no beginning
no simple instant
there is now
            and now
        and
    now

        no fire
is in the flame.

Old Houses

Old houses were scaffolding once
and workmen whistling,
nails whistling into the timber
a tune that didn't include us
who live now between these walls

raised by leathery hands
scarred by lessons learned the hard way,
hands twisting wire
tightening round an icy wrench,
finally relaxed

hands like petals
cupped round a match
to light a cigarette.
Old houses whistle now
in the winter wind

as workmen once on scaffolding
whistled
a tune that doesn't include us
who afterward call this house
our own.

Upas

(from *The Book of Trees*)

I read in the book of trees
of a certain tropical conifer
whose needles gleam in even
a moonless night and cast
no shadow in the light of day,
a tree that hides from you every
sorrow that has followed you all
these years.

Cut it down
with saw or axe and the sap
runs red, then all
the shadows it has hoarded flow into you.

All you will feel is a chill
as dark roots tighten
round your heart.

Gift

I sat frowning down coffee
at the bar and grill
when a pale man in a raincoat
walked in and stared around.
He was looking for someone
ignoring empty booths and stools.
He even for a moment
studied my face.

When he left I noticed
on the counter beside me
a small cardboard box
that I slipped in my pocket
on my way out.
Inside just a seashell
that gathers dust now on my mantel.

But sometimes when insomniac
I roam the night
the almost audible
words of a song
blow faintly through the house.

Flames on the Water

1

You were water, you ran away to earth
I ran after you, asking your immemorial secrets
You were water, you soaked me, carved my stone features,
ran away to the earth
I ran after you, praising your mind and heartless lens
You were water, you flowed from my eyes in convulsions,
ran away to the earth
I ran after you, ran away to the earth, but didn't find you
You slid away through a crack where I couldn't follow
I stood looking after you, sniffing the air

2

This flame goes out walking,
the flame at the base of the spine
begs along the street –

give me fuel, let me
burn you in my fire,
let me shine

3

You are fire, you leap to the sky
I leap after you, certain you know the way
You are fire, burning in my blood, you leap to the sky
I leap after you, leap to the sky and am lost
I stare after you, burning away so far as I
distill
            precipitate

Names, Faces, Rooms

over old snapshots
a girl looking up

> *or did I invent it, did nobody say it*
> *did you comb your hair, and did I watch*

where once in the outskirts, I saw a girl

> *dressed in my wishes you go naked*
> *you uproot my memory, your name I can't recall*

a trick of the mind
I walk all night in the wind

> *did you comb your hair, and did I watch*

tomorrow, yesterday, names, faces

> *a thought made flesh, the flesh sprouting wings*

the room bright with spring,
window spattered with rain, door open to the sea

> *the looks you give me rain all night*

the day ends, the year ends

> *no one is where I left them*

all of them, or none, a pencil point broken off

> *one glimpse of her eyes*
> *over old snapshots*

combing her hair, singing beside me

those two taking their clothes off,
those two kissing, naked before time

furnished rooms, city streets, names like wounds

each night the first night
faces crumbling in memory

looking into each other's eyes

her face is all faces, all her names are one name

looking up through the years

or did I invent it, did nobody say it
did you comb our hair, and did I watch

rooms, stains on the wall

those two taking their clothes off, those two

tomorrow, yesterday, names, faces
rooms adrift between cities, always at sea,
each room at the world's core

each night the first night

where love is a struggle
a thought made flesh, the flesh sprouting wings

the looks you give me rain

a girl leaning over her balcony, out into the rain

one of us said, or neither, did you
or did I invent it, did nobody say it

rooms adrift between cities, silent as waves in mid-ocean, sargasso
each night the first night

> *the looks you give me*

crumbling in memory

> *her name I forget, all her names*

tomorrow, yesterday, names, faces,
rooms

> *or did I invent it, did nobody say*

Transfer Expired

I hope you'll take me

Not today's color, no, but see
it's for this line

same day, same time of day

A year ago I was

waylaid by adventure or
marriage or paying work and
I never saw another bus go by

till you came along just now

It's all I have
to take me away

Famous Lovers

their fame has a long way to go
before it is really immortal
                    Rilke

And if they knew
the moment eternity twisted down
and picked them up together

if they knew how far they had to go
how they had to suffer
parted   persecuted   mocked   mortified

if they knew for what charm
of their perishing flesh
or what miracle by their grave

they were to be blessed   adored   beatified
could they suffer more gladly
their lovers' torments?

Not Time's Fool

When forty winters shall besiege thy brow
and dig deep trenches in thy beauty's field
Shakespeare

1

At forty, you're beautiful. Your child's
callow face is no more than a sketch
life will fill in, in good time;
but you're the portrait now, posed on a hill
amid ripening fields. That you have lived
is clear, but your blood is hot for more,
for the unfulfilled
ambitions, lusts, plans you shelved awhile
but – surprised? – did not forget. Look –
their traces remain, you can't erase them
if you try. And would you? You want
and, wanting, place yourself in the foreground
of a landscape overgrown with shadows
only your brush stroke can define.

2

You know every crop, each fruit has its brief
mellow season. Like Cézanne, you
study color, light and shade, the balance
of ripeness and decay. Your canvas
glows; the sky for an hour past sunset
strives to reflect that earthly grace
in vain. Stars burn long, but with a cold
hard light; your place is not among them.
All flesh is grass – you laughed at that once.
But in the waning light look back
to your own face in the mirror – those lines
that shadows darken round your eyes. You know
one morning you will wake, look out
and see first frost whitening the fields.

3

When I speak of you of course I mean
myself as well; you've seen
my red beard gray. Half yours, half mine –
this lifetime we have spent together;
and still, weary at the end of day,
we hurry to our bed. It's hard
to turn our minds to sleep;
tomorrow may be too late for this.
Or if you do turn in at pumpkin time
I'll often, like tonight,
turn on the light again, prolong
the day in writing lines we'll read
in grayer years, remembering
how once we made the darkness glow.

4

What a glorious morning it is
to spend between sweaty sheets.
The sun colors our walls through prisms
hung in the window. Outside
it makes the yellow maples shine,
dries the dew in the fading garden. But look –
we have leaves to rake, flowerboxes
to bring in so our winter
will be brightened by some of this
abundance. Time is short.
Today is Sunday; by next weekend
there may be snow. So rise my love.
Tonight we'll light the candles and
the windows of our room will sweat.

5

Well, in days like these an hour of joy
is much, though it brings disarmament
no closer; jails no child molester;
deters no grafter from seeking office,
winning a cabinet post and then,
when caught, becoming a director
of a Crown corporation; though it won't
cure AIDS, make virtue triumph, foil
the Contras or the ayatollahs
or the SDI; though the image,
not the policies, elects our leaders,
and the image, well manipulated,
lies; still an hour of joy is much
to find in our harried lives.

6

There have been hours, I admit, and years
our life didn't run on rails. It's true
I've hurt you. Worse: I've hurt you knowing
how betrayal hurts; how near
the double solid line I drove and how
the drug I was on impairs the sense;
how often innocent passengers
are injured worst. But that
won't bear retelling or remembering.
We both lived recklessly, on credit,
when the interest rate was high –
but close that account. No wrong
can ever repay another
and once forgiven no debt is owed.

7

There's a game you used to play in school:
first pupil finished an assignment,
you'd stare at the hour hand on the clock
to catch it moving; you'd try to
trick it, trip it – telekinesis! –
forward to three-thirty. Now
you'd slow it if you could; you swim
and work out to keep your figure.
But you're not fooled by the experts
who turn back the doomsday clock;
you've seen in satellite photos
the dark line of night sweep smoothly
across time zones. Watch with me
awhile longer, then, good night.

Through and Through

1

Many a chess master has wriggled on Morton's fork: bishop threatens both opposing knights – forks them. It is a mid-game move, named for the grandmaster of his time, Thomas Morton, Archbishop of Canterbury, who as Chancellor to Henry the Seventh fattened the royal treasury this way.

To the first knight: "I see you've taken on new men, bought them new livery, had repairs done around the castle. You must have plenty for the King." To the second knight: "I notice you're quite a miser, never waste a penny on luxuries. You must be saving a bundle for the King." Check and check; you're forked.

It goes without saying, he operated in the black.

2

My grandfather Morton would have frowned on such accounting. But though he was a scrupulous clerk with a head for figures, he somehow lost count of the generations since the first Morton arrived from south of the Great Lakes – surely the latest of the Loyalists.

3

Morton. The name meant death to the Cherokee who, when a Morton was Indian Commissioner, were force-marched from Tennessee beyond the Mississippi. De Tocqueville, passing through Memphis at the time, observed "they no longer have a country, and soon they will not be a people . . . *le souvenir même de leur nom s'est effacé; leurs langues sont perdues, leur gloire s'est évanouie comme un son sans écho.*"

4

Much later my parents, understanding neither French nor German, gave me the
name Todd Morton and expected me to live with it.

5

One morning my wife changed her name back to her father's, not mine
anymore. When we got married, she explained, she was young and didn't know
what a mistake it was to discard her identity. So when, renewing her driver's
license, she came to the line on the form for her name, she simply decided.

It is easier to change your name than your address. Nothing gets lost in the mail.
But I'm not so readily shaken.

A few months later, she went to a specialist because of her flat, aching feet. The
foot doctor took one look and swore, "Why didn't you come to me years ago?
Now the damage is done. See this hardening on the middle toe where all your
weight has crushed it? That's a condition called Morton's foot."

6

Morton. The word sounded like a wounded calf when my grandmother cried it,
the time she found my wife and me arguing.

It was a stupid quarrel; I mean, I was in the wrong. And my grandmother didn't
help matters, offering her sympathy. So I stormed from the room, stubborn as
any Morton faced with defiant knight or Indian.

"Oh dear, you have a tough row to hoe," she told my wife, and she should
know, having seen what her daughter went through, married to my father. "Oh,
he's a Morton through and through."

The Mother's Mark

1

Among brushes and powders on her mirrored dresser, my mother kept a photograph of me, age four, barefoot in overalls, face shaded by a broad straw hat. A young Huck Finn, someone called me, looking at that picture; but my mother must have been reminded of her father, with a pitchfork in his hand at haying time. She ordered prints for all the relatives and, for herself, a color copy.

Back in those mid-century, pre-Kodachrome days, portrait photographers pleased their customers by coloring prints by hand. So my denim overalls came out scuffless, my hair silver-blond, my face clean of all but a shadow of the portwine stain that covered my left cheek at birth.

There must have been many who, glancing at me and turning away embarrassed, wished to have that photographer's crayon, so they too could wash away, or at least not see, that mark that disturbed them. It shamed them to think it was the reason they shunned me.

2

Children were less self-conscious. "Who gave you the black eye?" they asked in all innocence, and were confused when their parents scolded them.

3

Once, though, on a German streetcar, it was the children in the back seat who were embarrassed, an old man who taunted me. A war veteran, no doubt, he must have mistaken me for an American, with my blue jeans and packsack. Remembering, perhaps, his own house destroyed by a bomb, flesh of his flesh scorched and scarred, he hectored me drunkenly. Understanding well enough, though we had no language in common, I sat there denying: "Nothing. Nothing happened to me." I have no one to blame for the marks I wear, which anyway, are only on the surface.

4

Someone, no doubt a great sinner, called it the mark of Cain.

5

In Poland, I'm told, it is called the kissing spot. There, children like me, cherished as gifts of God, are kissed and kissed with no fear of leaving lipstick marks.

My mother too, in her undemonstrative, Canadian way, cherished me. The year I started school, she took down my retouched photo from its place among creams and lotions and replaced it with a more recent snap – slightly overexposed, a gleam of light reflecting from my crimson cheek.

The Heart Is a Muscle

The heart is a muscle
It has to be strong
Go to the club every week
Give it a workout
Work it out   If you can
Give it a rubdown

If the heart were strong as steel
It would be stainless
Rub it down and it would shine
Give it a rubdown
Rub it on stone   If you can
Give it a sharp edge

If the heart were a knife
It would be deadly
You would hone it and sheath it
Keep it hidden
You'd feel safe just knowing
It was on you

But the heart is a muscle
One day it will fail you
Give it a workout   a rubdown
Keep it sharp
But don't think it will save you
It's only your heart

Love's Body

Even a brief absence is a season
out of time. For a week
I'm a single parent — women glance
and ask if I have custody — while you
eat at tables for one, choose hotels
with pools and saunas, relearn
double-entendres like travel advance.

Last month, our places reversed.
No departure times or cab receipts
you marked your days in naps, floor games
loads of laundry while I did lunch
for the good of — not the waist — the bottom line
and boogied the night away
with the hotel's remote control.

Tomorrow is another day. We'll meet
at the airport and make the exchange:
I'll rescue your case from the carrousel
while you pick up the talkative baggage
we carry our love in, kiss *him* first,
our eyes entwined not in each other's
but on the body of our love —
who will wake us — together — in the morning.

Royal Garden Hotel

yesterday's snow storm on the 401 and today's
rhodendrons on English Bay   erect cones of
blossoms on the chestnut trees   between them
the distance I travelled without telling you
the distance we travelled together   the place
we called home the place we went toward even
if it wasn't there until we got there   if I say
remember when we drove in fog   even if there
was fog with the snow yesterday on the 401
even if fog hung over English Bay this morning
obscuring the mountains you will remember the
New Years we skiied in the Rockies   returning
through fog so thick I stopped the car in the
driving lane of the TransCanada and walked
forward knowing I would still see nothing and
walked back thinking this is the stupidest thing
I have ever done   any minute another car may
explode out of the fog   and this morning
another H-bomb sank to the bottom of the
ocean and something fell out of the sky and
landed on the car beside me   I walked up and
down the corridors looking for ice in this hotel
where the soap disappears after every use and I
wonder if this is assurance   the H-bombs too
might disappear   I mean the ones on the ocean
floor   the distance too the distance I travelled
without you   the distance too might end on the
ocean floor   where it never freezes and there is
no fog or light

Eclipse

(for Jeffrey)

Way past midnight
I wake you, brushing fingers
across your gleaming forehead,
slide you into slippers
and steer you outside

        Night roses, pale red echoes
        of the moon's blue,
        blown lilac scent,
        deep sigh of a city asleep

Grandmother, mother, father and son,
we bundle in blankets,
pace the backyard with hands in pockets,
as the moon, ripening, reddening,
enters earth shadow

Before the end it is gray as a cloud
but, straight from dreams, you're not easily impressed
Your grandmother's smiling eyes
excite you more than the smoked-glass
ghost of a moon up there

and down here in the grass!
Gleefully you cup your hands
round a fading light

and later, when you crayon a picture of the eclipse
you call it, The Night I Saw the Glow-worms.

Comet
Music

George Frederick Handel's Comet Music (1759)

My countryman Dr. Halley says
it's only gas and ice
and plots its course among the stars
like a cargo of tea and rice.

But last night I saw it rising
beyond the Windsor Forest
as I lifted my gaze to give the cue
for the Hallelujah chorus.

> A great white grace note
> sprayed across the skies,
> a crystal invitation
> to improvise.

Had not the king been in his throne,
his eyes in a glassy stare,
I'd have jumped down from the podium,
told them all to turn their chairs

and under my direction
read the music in the skies.
They'd have filled the royal darkness
with the glory in my blind eyes.

Hallelujah. Hallelujah?
That was only my first try.
The music I write next time
will make the chorus fly.

Halleylujah! Halleylujah!
The heavenly host will all join in.
Halley   lujah!

Mémoires d'un amnésique

(improvisations on themes by Erik Satie)

Trois sarabandes

The fire smoulders, then catches,
flickers, and just when you think

it's dying away, another flare
rises toward the dusky sky.

Fancy footwork, how a stream
picks its way down a hillside

exposing nuggets where you saw
only grit and clay

then spreads in a pool
that catches the sky in its gaze.

A few steps, a lovely phrase,
then pull up short, begin again.

This must be the Andalusian melody
to which the lobsters dance.

Trois gymnopédies

Sun. The mild summer of Normandy. Bees hovering over fields of sweet clover. Breezes barely disturb the high branches of willow. Clouds slowly swell, slowly turn. The scent of cut grass, soft mud of river banks.

All the long afternoon the mind wanders. A leaf gently buoyed on the stream. Even the songbirds rest in the shade. Sluggish ants return to their cool lairs. A swan gliding on the pond dips its head.

Now shadows lengthen. A chill falls over the river bank. Reluctantly the wanderer rises, stretches, looks across the fields toward home, and there the sunset turns the bleached barn gold.

Trois gnossiennes

Three women of Knossos
making olive oil.
These women of Knossos
never tire of toil.

They shake the branches of the trees
and then get down upon their knees.
They sort the ripe from rotten from green,
the most beautiful women I've ever seen.

From this fort upon the hill
a ruler once enforced his will,
and in his prison, its belly full
of Athenian blood, he kept a bull.

We'll never see such a king again
for this is now and that was then.

Deux pièces froides

How different the scene looks, covered in snow. We must imagine the streams running on beneath the ice. Cool as a sherbet in July, without the strong sun to make dew bead on the glass.

How slowly we lumber across the fields, wearing hides on our backs and strips of woven hide on our feet. Hidden, all the fur-bearing life we used to glimpse, dodging between the trees. All asleep now. No songbirds; only the hoarse croak of the raven. Its black eye spying on us.

Not too far, now. Don't wander away. You know how the wind can turn you around in a minute. How the snow can make the familiar strange. How night can creep up in mid-afternoon. Think of the crackling fire at home, the smell of cedar and pine sap boiling.

Trois morceaux en forme de poire

This is the shape of mystery.

You'd think, like the avocado, it would have a large, impenetrable pit, from which a periscope projects to spy on the world. But no. Cut into it, it gives way. Its flesh is like your own would be, when ripe — little grainy pores, succulent, flavoured of sunshine. Juice dribbles down your chin, but you eat on without pause, as if it's a summer day inserted into February. You'd like to eat it all, even the tiny, sprightly seeds that jump from between your fingers.

But ah, there is mystery after all. Not in the shape, but in the way it continues to appeal, even when you are surfeited. How it makes you want more. How it leaves you dissatisfied with the way you are, yearning for a knowledge only hinted at in its tissue-thin layer of skin. This must be the fruit that Yahweh forbade to Adam and Eve. The fruit the Olympians eat, not because they are hungry, but because they want to be human.

Embryons desséchés

The waning sea leaves them
among starfish and barnacles
where tide pools used to be.

Dig in the sand and you'll find them
desiccated, forlorn, dreaming
of the lives they might have led.

High tide, and other spawn swarm over them.
Sea horses gallop on the foam,
full of themselves, no care in the world.

They rattle on the pebble beach,
the waves, in full crescendo,
mindless of the new moon coming.

Descriptions automatiques

Click-wind, click-wind, click-wind, click-wind. No need to adjust the shutter.
Take snaps all round, three-sixty degrees, and later, when I find these shots in a
drawer, I'll forget where I was, what I was thinking of, if anything at all, and
delight in imagining what these are pictures of, and where, and whose character
I assumed this day out of time, when you'd say I wasn't myself.

Avant-dernières pensées

The newsmen show them all lined up –
the tides, the new moon, the end of holy days.
What they cannot show we dream for ourselves –

the enemy in their bunkers, hunkered
cold and hungry; afraid, we hope,
afraid as we are of the fire at our backs.

It's no idyll – this desert sunrise – the wind
that brings, we hope, no more than dust
to clog our deadly machines, our eyes.

Rêverie (*one of* Trois petites pièces montées)

The clock, the clock, tick-a-tock.
Why doesn't it leap and sway
the way I feel today?

Tick-a-tock, tick-a-tock, little friend.
Won't you syncopate a song
while you plod along?

Aperçus désagréables

It is for such things you wait.
For such things you endure the tedium
of passing years. You lay up,
as they say, you lay up plans.
Strange to say then, when the day
has come – strange, I say,
to be so little moved. To feel,
how shall I say? a slight
nausea, no, revulsion
now the waiting is done.

Sonatine bureaucratique

Funny little guy. Does he know
what his mustache will mean
to a later generation? More,
no doubt, than all the official papers
that cover his desk. But ah,
he has a pure heart; who
could fail to love his little soul?

Croquis et agaceries d'un gros bonhomme

See how he looks at you sideways?
He thinks you're making fun of the way he walks.
And who could resist?

Now look – his huge handkerchief –
how carefully he folds it
after blowing his nose with a honk.

Could he have lived in any other time?
Could he wear sneakers, say, instead of spats?
A Blue Jays cap in place of his bowler? No?

Well wait till his shift at the theme park is done,
then see him in a beer-stained sweat shirt
stocking up at the liquor store.

La belle excentrique

She thinks she is a dancer. Ignoring
the image in her mirror, she steps

on the tips of her fat toes, wiggles
fat fingers at the clouds tripping by.

Ah, moon, she sings, *you are my one
true love, most constant admirer.*

*I will dance for you, alone,
for you alone appreciate me.*

*The Royal Winnipeg will never know
the beauty that might have graced its boards.*

*Kiss my eyelids, here, just here
in my suburban backyard*

*we need fear no intruders. They
are only jealous, but you'll see,*

*I'll watch for you each night,
and when you come I'll dance*

*for you alone, on the tips of my toes,
on the chilly, dew-soaked grass.*

She whirls and whirls in her filmy
night dress, arms wide open

to the silver, smiling moon.

Auditory Camouflage

that cow you just heard is meaowing in a tree

      a stampede of elephants
      preens its feathers

you have sighted the liarbird
so named for its tail
which looks like a lyre
and because its call is

          crickets

   thunder

             balalaikas

    drops of water

from **The Still Point**

quaking
            lightening
                        storming
the world hangs
            by the thread
                        of a nerve

it is blue
            it is gibbous and
                        crescent and half and full
in the skies of the planets
            it spins
                        in their clouds
it spins in the minute
            dancing inside
                        the inside the
minute suspended
            on the crest
                        of a wave
when you cupped
            the sun in your hands
                        and threw it out of time

it spins
            in a water drop
                        arcing through light

in the fluid kick of cell
            in the hook of claw
                        on the crest of a wave
rising
            to an ice-edged
                        wind

in the unfolding lily
      still under water
             that hangs by the thread
of the timeless
      minute
          inside time

silence rings   rings of sound
surround   the horizon
rising   singing
drops of sound   burst
on the surface   of time

seconds suspended   drops blown outward
rise   arc
reflecting   each
a perfect   red
sun

for an instant after impact
the glass does not shatter

          for an instant
          there is no sound

for an instant
at the height of her dive

          the diver is motionless
          may fly away
                  into

Instant On

1

I'm instant on. You press
and between us particles charge

and discharge instantly.
Eyewitness, you say, be

up to the minute
in living color,

more, be true, be
my window, be my eyes.

2

Unblinking, I do what I can.
But to show you truly

things as they are
is not in my circuits

nor part of the signal
I pull from the air.

Red clouds, a bright green sky,
jade ocean, olive flesh

of dancing maidens, these
are effortless achievements.

But is this all you ask of me?
To say this is all,

is things as they are,

to braid my beam into this
nightmare paradise, cartoon grin,
the loud slurred voice

of public opinion,
a world in your grasp.

3

But things as they are cannot be
compact into minute spots.

Though factory adjusted, my black
can never be black, my skies

do not sing, my seas are not cold
and do not cleanse.

Radiation is all
I really touch you with.

Imperceptibly the stream of particles
representing an island becomes

the island itself, clarified.
The world itself desires

such a transubstantiation.
Olive skin becomes blue

red and yellow spots fired
on a treated surface. I am

the image you have made, and you
are what the image has made you.

4

What an age sits quietly forgetting
there in the wintry blue

is all their mothers ever knew,
the time bread takes to rise,

how to make a bed and
lie in it, lies more true

than things as they are,
the uses of truth,

the chosen dreams, the rare
and risky act of choice.

Hymn of Thanks

(to my PC)

Thank you
silent partner
faithful co-ordinator
meticulous savior of my least vision or revision
fellow slave of stray thoughts at all hours

Thank you, alert one
for your gentle tutelage
your mild reminder to save
replace
to call everything by its name

Thank you for your patience
your reassuring chuckle while saving
your modest advice
memos   appointments   things to do
lists carried over day by day until done

Thank you for your ever-wakefulness
for simple queries
like "Delete to end of page?"
and for the undelete key
for your silent reminder to save again

Thank you for your nanosecond speed
and for the lesson
I am so slow to learn:
no matter how far I progress each day
always to back up at night.

Night Light of the Soul

All night the minutes drip silently into the liquid crystal of St. John's digital watch. On the screen the cursor awaits the next output of his soul. Far below, the thermostat fires up the furnace, while the traffic light outside his window switches from green to amber to red. Any minute a power surge may wipe out his last hour's illumination, but meanwhile, his file is saved; the wordwrap function automatically hyphenates Purgatory.

An Artist Contemplates Her Sketches

These few lines – tried
over and over – essayed and found wanting
 – plotted on the map of page
again and again in changing figures:
I look at them now and, like my sister
with her teenage sons, can't believe
they all came out of me.

First, the sleek flanks of galloping horses
vaulting fences, gates, crevasses,
fast – caught fast in time –
inertia kills them.
                              Here
pared down, unpolished, unprimed,
unsweated – a mere
                    contrivance of lines – machine
                              of balanced tensions
                                        reduced
to a valentine heart – a cartoon
bosom – swollen nipples – hard
breast unsuckled.
Now shaded, round faces at breasts
 – round hands and bellies
that would be pink if my horse-hair
brushes weren't herded away.

It's the soft pencil my hand caresses today.
It breeds these round hungry mouths,
mewling, crying to be
fed into this world,
suck the sweet fluid
of mine into their carbon one.

How it hurts! The blood moving
in these dead parts, the salt
taste in my mouth.
My blunt pencil slowly
leaks darkness onto the page
 – greedy hands, hungry mouths.
Give! they cry. Give! My hand
moves, strokes, but can't satisfy.
My swollen, empty belly cries –

Two Authors in Search of a Character

When they met the page was already written.
They read daylight between the lines.
They wrote cross-hatched, met in the middle
And comma'd the paper with sighs.

Their child was born with ink in its veins
And only a paper heart.
The critics told them no hope remained
Unless one of them gave up the art.

He loved her denouements, said he,
Far more than any others.
But his were books of Poetry,
And babies need their mothers.

His words were blue as ice, said she,
While hers burned scarlet red.
Unless *he* became an employee
Their child would soon be dead.

The child was neither boy nor girl.
It had an inhuman look.
Since it died a babe, the rest of the world
Has to read of it in a book.

Table Games

The Chess Table

Was used for jigsaws   in summer
When the children came to stay
And once made do   when you taught me Othello

And Pente   that elegant game
Of pairs   We played with pennies
Dull versus shiny   on the corners of the squares

The Tablemen

Came wrapped with a bow   under the tree
Sixteen of ebony   as many of ivory
Or cedar and pine?   Memory like an army

Hides its stratagems   But those chiseled kings
Had little choice   To hide behind their castles
Or advance to face their foes

Table Wine

Pour!   don't be slow
Let tomorrow go hang
Shake the walls   with laughter

Friends!   a toast
For the first time in years   maybe the last
We are all sitting down together

Appelles' Table

Bacchus laughs   blue eyelids drooping
Grapes in his hair   His belly
Hangs into his plate
                    Turn tables
And a maiden reads her hymnary
Embroidered in gold   Only her left eye's
Sidelong glance reveals
                    the wheel is still turning

The Round Table

Merlin devised it   so none would be first
Good managers still   turn the trick
When odds are even   and no corners divide

They were pretty   those knights in armour
But when they left the table   they turned
On one another   themselves   and died

The Tablet

I play on it   with my pen
My eyes play over   its tableau
Tabula rasa   Four corners

Nothing more   An open field
Where shadows play   till these accounts are tabled
And I turn the page

Prayers at Table

The Lord gave us to eat   made us welcome
At His table   Turned water into wine
In the desert   drank from a stone

Though like God   we no longer listen
To our prayers   we sit in silence
Grateful for this gift

Running the Table

Some could do it   From a clean break
sink every red ball   then the yellow
Green brown blue and pink in order

Finally pocket the black   with a solid thud
A cocky half-look back   at the startled faces
Then shake a curl of hair   across the forehead

Winning Against the Table

Requires patience   a good hand
And a poker face   Win big once
And you're spoiled for life

You're too quick   with your bets
Try to stare down   the Queen of Hearts
You bluff   You fall for bluffs

On the Operating Table

The drug lowers you slowly   a lure on a hook
Into your body's   dark waters
You can't feel the cool fingers   the deep sharp blade

It's too late for excuses   You sink
Deeper   toward the other shore
Where you will wake up   changed

Tabulation

When all is told   the numbers look bare
In their   precarious balance
Another tally   won't alter

This nagging doubt   that all is not told
Nor equal the sum   that fills the blank space
In the bottom line

Endymion's Dream

(London, 1815)

At dawn I wake cold and alone
to the sound of Bow bells
echoing off the embankment
where youth lies eyeless
in the vomit on the alley stones

I rise with the stink from the gutter
lifting eyes beyond rooftops
toward the pale, sickly moon

go coughing through murky streets
to set bones at the hospital
wash wounds with river water
hold down a screaming patient
while the surgeon cuts

Opium!
the poor beggar cries

Give me a dream

Letters from Kentucky

My dear George,

I shall in a short time write you as far as I know
how I intend to pass my Life –
I cannot think of those things
now Tom is so unwell and weak.

Notwithstanding your Happiness and your recommendation
I hope I shall never marry.
Though the most beautiful Creature were waiting for me
at the end of a Journey or a Walk;
though the carpet were of Silk,
the Curtains of the morning Clouds;
the chairs and Sofa stuffed with Cygnet's down;
the food Manna,
the Wine beyond Claret,
the Window opening on Winander mere,
I should not feel – or rather
my Happiness would not be so fine,
as my Solitude is sublime.

The roaring of the wind is my wife and
the Stars through the window pane are my Children
I feel more and more every day,
as my imagination strengthens,
that I do not live in this world alone
but in a thousand worlds.

31 October 1818

Dear brother,

By now you will know
our ship docked safely in Philadelphia.
On the seas our future was in His hands –
Upon land we must learn self-reliance.

Having inquired for the stage to Pittsburgh
and finding there was none,
I inquired no further into why
(no roads worthy the name)
but put down hard money for wagon and horse and set out,
little George at my side,
to cross the Allegheny mountains.

To you it is but an outlandish name –
and was to us till this past month
which we thank God to have survived.
Had I your fluid tongue
I could describe you gorges, cataracts, flocks and herds
sublime enough to fill your mightiest poem.

Being thus far spared
I have every faith we will succeed.
Never again need I beg Mr. Abbey
for a place on a junior clerk's stool.

This morning we board an Ohio steamer
bound five hundred miles downstream
to Birkbeck's settlement.

Our best to Tom and all our friends.

October 1818

My dear Brother and Sister,

You will have been prepared, before this reaches you
for the worst news you could have.

The last days of poor Tom were most distressing;
but his last moments were not so painful,
and his very last was without a pang.

I will not make parsonic comments on death —
yet the common observations of the commonest people
are as true as their proverbs.

December 1818

Dear brother,

We have had no word of you since we departed.
One letter only, from Georgiana's mother, found us
at Birkbeck's – a fine site of rich farms,
mills, stores, stills, printing presses.
But as we are latecomers, we found
no cleared land to buy at any price –
the oak and elm forest so deep
that even the light of noon
seems remote as England.

In short, we have moved on.
But think it no loss –
as if Abbey had argued away in Chancery
our whole inheritance. Here one mischance
opens on new opportunity.
On the steamboat I met a fine man –
an artist and writer
whose punning high spirits remind me of you.
Now this gentleman, Mr. Audubon,
daily expects a river freighter
loaded to the gunnels with cloth and such goods
so much in demand in these growing towns
that fine profits are assured – and mark you
this Audubon requires a partner!

Tonight I pledge the best part of my guineas
for a share in that cargo,
which may double my money tomorrow.
Make no mistake – this land holds no terror
for the bold, only rich rewards.

Write care of J.J. Audubon,
Henderson, Kentucky

December 1818

My dear Brother & Sister –

How are you going on now?
The going on of the world makes me dizzy –
There you are with Birkbeck – here I am with Brown –
sometimes I fancy an immense separation,
and sometimes, as at present,
a direct communication of Spirit with you.

I remember your Ways and Manners and actions;
I know your manner of thinking, your manner of feeling:
I know what shape your joy or your sorrow would take;
I know the manner of your walking, standing, sauntering, sitting down,
laughing, punning, and every action so truly
that you seem near to me.
You will remember me in the same manner –
and the more when I tell you
that I shall read a passage of Shakespeare
every Sunday at ten o'Clock –
you read one at the same time
and we shall be as near each other
as blind bodies can be in the same room.

December 1818

Dear brother,

This evening, opened Shakespeare thinking of you
and fell upon your favourite play
"that fierce dispute
Betwixt damnation and impassion'd clay"
and the words burned up at me –
"Poor Tom's a-cold"

Such dread I have this Christmas eve.
Tonight "the foul fiend haunts poor Tom
in the voice of a nightingale"
and I fear for him.

Are we all miscarried, John, or soon to be?
Like you I fear an early death
awaits us all – Our family was always phlegmatic
sluggish, lazy, fancy-free
but we with our lofty ambitions
must burn ourselves up like the phoenix
in a few years' industry.

In this labour a wife is a great strength –
I mean an even-tempered wife like mine,
who suffers gracefully
the hardships that surprise us daily.

Older brother, since you are unmarried
you are in some ways my junior in experience.
Take this advice –
Marry, and soon, a good strong girl.
Failing that employ the services
of a lady of the night (for the good of your health
become a regular at an established house).
It will do you no end of good
in the regulation of your blood.

December 1818

My dear Brother & Sister –

How is it we have not heard from you from the Settlement yet?
The letters must surely have miscarried.
I am in expectation every day –

Circumstances are like Clouds
continually gathering and bursting –
While we are laughing the seed of some trouble
is put into the wide arable land of events –
while we are laughing it sprouts it grows
and suddenly bears a poison fruit
which we must pluck –

I go among the Fields and catch a glimpse of a Stoat
or a fieldmouse peeping out of the withered grass –
the creature hath a purpose and its eyes are bright with it.
I go amongst the buildings of a city
and I see a Man hurrying along – to what?
the Creature has a purpose and his eyes are bright with it.

But then, as Wordsworth says, "we have all one human heart" –
there is an electric fire in human nature
tending to purify – so that among these human creatures
there is continually some birth of new heroism.
The pity is that we must wonder at it:
as we should at finding a pearl in rubbish.

March 1819

Dear brother,

I feel your misfortune the more
for the freshness of my own
and curse the distance
that leaves us no help to each other.

In short, all my hopes have failed.
Mr. Audubon's boat, when he sold it to me,
sat on the bottom of the Ohio River.

Now my second boat too has run aground
I had resolved to sue (a common resort
among speculators) when I learned
Mr. Audubon's quicker creditors cleaned him out.
He resides in jail now, and much subdued
he resolves to give up business
and devote himself to drawing woodland birds –
So long as he bankrupt only himself with them.

Never mind, I will go out
and shoot our supper – No one's to stop me –
No, they'll respect me the more.

I have no intention of failing
but ask of you this –
Go to Mr. Abbey
speak to him for me –
have him send the rest of my money!

May 1819

My dear George,

The first thought that struck me on reading your last,
was to mortgage a Poem to Murray:
but on more consideration
I made up my mind not to do so:

My name with the literary fashionables is vulgar –
I am a weaver boy to them –

I feel I can bear any thing – any misery, even imprisonment –
so long as I have neither wife nor child.
Perhaps you will say yours are your only comfort –
they must be

I have pass'd my time in reading, writing and fretting –
the last I intend to give up and stick to the other two.
They are the only chances of benefit to us.
Your wants will be a fresh spur to me.

From the time you left me,
our friends say I have altered completely –
am not the same person –
perhaps in this letter I am
for in a letter one takes up one's existence
from the time we last met –

We are like the relict garments of a Saint;
the same and not the same:
for the careful Monks patch it and patch it
till there's not a thread of the original garment left.

September 1819

John,

Georgiana's mother reports you have sailed for Italy.
Bravo!
I suppose you will see great opera
whether you go to Milan or stay in Rome –
You must write and tell me.
The Great Sandini sang in Louisville Saturday
but he had a great head cold and sang badly
for under an hour.

I hope your health responds to the Mediterranean
as your imagination always has.
For God's sake don't let stormy seas,
cramped quarters, poor and little food defeat you.
Remember how you endured the years at Guy's
– applying leeches, setting bones –
no matter how you hated it you saw it through.

So I've had to do –
But are we afraid? We are not!
I've bought a mill on a slope where ten years hence
you will see only houses built with my wood.

O brother!
what killed Tom is killing you and will kill me.
Call it what you will, it is consuming us.
Shall one of our family make a success for us all?
I promise, as long as I live
your poems will be loved
in the heart of America.

I send this with Sandini's troupe –
I know not how it will ever reach you.

September 1820

(In May 1818, at the age of twenty-one, George Keats, brother of the poet, married Georgiana Wylie and emigrated to America where, after an unfortunate partnership with the not-yet-famous John James Audubon, he eventually amassed a fortune as owner of lumber and grain mills. His home in Louisville, Kentucky, became a center of local literary activity until his death at forty-four of tuberculosis, the disease that had killed his brothers.

Excerpts from letters of John Keats to his brother are in italics. The letters from George were not saved and exist only in imagination. John and George Keats were the oldest of four orphaned children. Their brother Tom died in 1818; their sister Fanny, still a child at that time, lived with their guardian, Richard Abbey, who mishandled the children's inheritance and hid its full extent from them.)

The History of
the Future Tense

The History of the Future Tense

Is it too late then
            or too early
to begin to write the history
            of the future tense?

            I
      you
            he she
      we they
            it.

Lions tear prey from
            their own cubs' mouths.
Tortoises
            heave in a limbic fog.
But who comes after
            to dig up the eggs?

      Will
            will
      will will
            will will
      will.

And how
      unless we remember
can we ever make it
            new?

Piledriver

                                        B-BOOM

A piledriver pierces frozen earth
where lately Neilsen's kitchen was

                                        B-BOOM

On the boulevard dogged walkers
lean into the wind
while a pile of bricks is ground to dust
by a bulldozer straining on chains
hooked to a naked windowframe
staring out on —

                        Rome
                        Babylon
                        Nineveh
            All shattered

                                        B-BOOM

                    Cairo
                    Sidon
            Who could name them all?

And we too – riding the streetcar
we have ridden for years
at this time of morning –
we go down among them
a few more each day
down among the untellable
        Clutching our color-coded transfers
        (valid till the end of the line)

In a café window breath steams
Fingers loosen round hot porcelain

B-BOOM

London
Vienna

Down go the old
the untellable cities

Up the unspeakable new

Waking Up in Guatemala

I am walking empty streets covered with fall leaves
but what I smell can't be from leaves alone – this fragrant rot

Unless it is the wind, I hear shots across town
unless it is the wind

I walk toward the river, intent
on reaching my friend's house near the bridge

I start to short-cut across a schoolyard, back away smartly
but not in time
At a glance I know those people
forcing three others to their knees with guns at their heads
don't want to stop at three

and one of them saw me

Now hiding is hopeless
My friends – to take me in will endanger them

Trying not to run
I circle a ruined house in the reeds by the river
then double back

A dark house
without heat
it is far from deserted

whole families hide here
bringing no safety in numbers

I know I must move on but –

and this is the part of the dream I can't quite remember

just how those families consoled me
made me feel safe enough to think of staying

how little by little I learned to trust
then to love those families hiding in the rushes
inhabiting abandoned houses, making them home

it's too simple – my escape – to wake in the morning
to a news report
leaving them there by the river while the death squads are out

Missing Person

Something was missing
What else could I do   I went looking

First I prayed to it   then
pointed a lens where I thought it should be

All along   taking notes   I made up theories
wrote them down and

kept on writing   inventing answers   destinations
until   old enough

(or almost)
I took pen and paper to the edge of the highway

and stood   thumb out
begging entry to dangerous dreams

myself a missing person now
with real destinations

lots of them   none
the one imagined

A Bouquet for Blaine

We meet by the escalator
as we have each week or so
for eight years now, at twelve-fifteen,
clutching our bag lunches for a brief
escape from telephones and deadlines.

We'd look for an empty park bench
and walk the riverbank we've both
written into our poems, but ice
still chokes the Ottawa and sidewalks
are perilous, so we cross the worn tiles
of the concourse between our office blocks,
past the fast food boutiques,
talking of last night's reading,
favorite books, the uncertain progress
of our poems through awkward drafts
toward their uncertain fate.

It's March, and I know you're impatient
to be turning the soil in the garden
you started with Kathleen the spring
you learned she was dying.
Within a year, you told me
as we headed toward the windows
overlooking the icy street,
the cancer tearing through her
like a weed would choke out her life.

But three years passed before the grim
November day you heaped flowers
on her coffin; three years of treatments,
side effects, nightmares you shared with me
through seasons of bag lunches,
walking the concourse between our buildings
or paths along the riverbank in spring,

high summer, dead of winter, spring again.
Toward the end we met more rarely,
or briefly at coffee-time,
your lunch hours, mornings, evenings
all spent at Kathleen's bedside,
planning new blooms for the garden
you knew she wouldn't live to see;
willing her two contradictory things:
the strength to go on; an easy death.

And driving home from the hospital
late at night, walking the riverbank
to work, even by the escalator
waiting for me at twelve-fifteen,
you were always brooding over
another new poem – a seed
of love nurtured by your grief.

Four more years have passed since the funeral,
and with patience few but gardeners
and poets would understand, you've gone on
weeding, cultivating, grooming those lines
with the care you once gave to her.

Today, the March sun has begun
to clear the ice from sidewalks,
bare the paths by the riverbank,
stirring life in bulbs beneath the soil,
and at last the fragrant leaves
of your book are opening –
a hardy variety that will bloom
for years in the hands of readers
not frightened by the knowledge
of all you lived through.

The Morning After

It was a cold December day, with fresh snow, and driving across the bridge into Quebec I was surprised at the heat, the devotion that must have kept the spray-painters going, the night before. Nearly every *ARRET/STOP* sign in sight had been painted — the *S* blacked out, and parts of the *T* and *P* — so all that remained of the English were the numbers **101**. I wondered if all the painters were tall enough to reach so high, or if they had taken stools with them, or if they had gone in pairs — a young woman, say, sitting on her boyfriend's shoulders — and whether she took her glove off to do the spraying. The vapor jet from those spray cans is cold at the best of times, and I supposed there were a few pairs of gloves that morning with black-painted fingertips.

A new restaurant had opened recently on Maisonneuve — the Thai Kitchen/ *Cuisine Thai* — and its signs had received a lot of black paint overnight. Across its white stucco the biggest **101** of all, in figures six feet high, greeted motorists as we came off the bridge. And in the square in front of the federal building, painters had written on the fibreglass sculpture *L'amour*, in English yet, "Anglos go home" — a challenging thought, both for the owners of the Thai Kitchen/ *Cuisine Thai* and for the Anglos whose ancestors homesteaded this province two centuries ago.

The pavement was icy, and it took special care not to fall flat as I crossed the square toward work. Though it wasn't easy to form a clear picture in my mind when I said the word *home*, I thought it an idea worth pursuing, at least as far as my desk. But while hanging up my coat and listening to my computer boot up, I remembered the French saying, no doubt a favorite with the spray-painters, *Qui ne dit rien, consent.* So I looked up the phone number for building maintenance, ready to lodge a complaint and have that illegal English sign removed. The line was busy, though, so I said to myself, *What the hell, I'll write something.*

For what seemed a long time after that, I stared at a blank computer screen with only a four-letter word on it — *h-o-m-e.*

1990

To remember without lying is difficult
          John Newlove

My country   he said   *my country*
and stared at the line of drink in his glass
not half   not even a quarter full.
Do you understand?   It's going to hell.

Then he swallowed and I   leaning forward
to hear above the party's din
was struck silent   as when a gust
from the opening door announces
the new arrival is winter
and a hush falls over the crowded room.

So I filled it   I filled his glass
though I knew   when he looks like this
it's best to call a cab.   *My country
is in pieces. Don't you understand?*

I nodded   cautiously   yes
though I knew   he is no exile
has no exile's   bitter-sweet memories
only today's rage   and an empty   glass.

I could call it my own   this land
of hard-riding desires he wrote of once
and it hurt to sit there   speechless
on the edge of my chair   dumbfounded
thinking of what we were to be
while he grew angry at my silence

thinking obscurely of the millions
who cry for their tortured countries now
late at night at parties in warm houses
like this one   each of us alone.

The Fall

Morning's red maples remember sunrise.
         Saudi Arabia / Kuwait
Birds on their perches waste no breath on flight
         Iran / Iraq / Kahnawake
till the moment is ripe. It's harvest time.
         Oka / Pretoria / Natal

Kahnawake / Haida / Temagami
         Kanesatake / Lubicon
Manitoba justice / Budget slashes
         Anishnabai / Manitoulin
The list is so long and so painful
         Shootout / Mixups / Under cover

People everywhere you look are fed up.
         The barricades demand respect.
At a famous man's funeral last week
         Sing the blues. Send in the army.
the CTV cameraman's T-shirt said
         "Clyde Wells for our Prime Minister."

Time will deceive you when you're not looking.
         Scatter the seeds in the open.
Raise the priority. Announce a truce.
         Drink the anniversary wine.
Full moon. The politicians want our votes.
         Socialist hordes are at the gate.

The earth quakes from Iran to Ecuador
         A toxic cloud over Ufa
Talks / Factions / Fallout in Mururoa
         Deadlines / Black death in Nairobi
Winds, floods, ideas, natural forces.
         Cooler. Diversify and wait.

Brothers

We ran the deer together
bivouacked above the river
drank lapsang souchong
with sugar before dawn
We crossed our two arms over
and called each other brother
Now the big man says *Stay there* to you
and tells me *Move along*

The big man says *Stay there* –
Or else is what you hear
He tells me *Stand aside*
my own business I should mind

But don't forget we ran the deer
though you stay there and I am here
It is time we made our stand
explain the truth to that big man

The Last Long Weekend

The last long weekend before the war
the sun rose over green fields and blue seas,
glass towers reflected its light by day and shone a bluish white at night
trains ran on time and nearly empty,
driving was permitted anywhere at any hour and everyone drove,
airports were twenty-four-hour shopping malls.

The last long weekend before the war the market was bullish.
The arms trade created a thousand new jobs and paid no taxes,
destinies hung on a half-cent rise or fall in the value of the dollar,
citizens complained of the tax on their income and property,
the price of the groceries that filled their carts,
workers went on strike to protect their pension funds from inflation
and saw themselves for the first time on television,
everyone took up yoga, jogging, drugs, cosmetics, registered charities,
letters to the editor, food food food,
deterrent was a household word,
knowing the closest to the blast die instantly without pain,
people crowded into cities and drove themselves into the ground.

The last long weekend faith made a comeback,
spring flowers grew,
dew drops clung to their petals,
reflecting in their tiny globes
the sun and earth and all.

The Comedy of Eras

No one found it very funny at the time. The post-cold war era blew into town on the winds of change and was promptly mistaken for its long-lost twin, which coincidentally went by the same name. There was bound to be confusion.

For the *familiar* post-cold war era was a fun-loving, free-spending, friendly sort of era, slightly rowdy but lovable. A carouser. It was famous for the time it got drunk and knocked down an old wall. As it happened, everyone agreed that wall was long overdue for knocking down. No harm done.

But the other era — the one we'll call the evil twin — simply didn't understand. It was a case of failure to discriminate. The evil twin seemed to want to knock *all* the walls down, and no one thought this funny at all.

Petty jealousies arose, and some not so petty. Everyone started calling in old debts. Fights broke out, and you know I don't mean fisticuffs. The line simply had to be drawn somewhere. It was no laughing matter.

Now it's time for the *deus ex machina:* a prime-time briefing with satellite feed. A recognition scene is called for; improbable revelations; hugs all round. The audience longs to heave a sigh of relief and be sent home laughing.

But post-cold war authors aren't keen on closure; we prefer the old rules, like old walls, broken. All plays, attentively read, are problem plays. Why shouldn't a comedy end with dead bodies littering the stage, providing the villain flees? Boundaries are for crossing.

For Now

They walk in and out of your life till
without noticing you begin to rely
on them, going in and out. You notice
when you realize some have gone
out of your life one last time and you
won't see them again, or if you do,
it is lifetimes later on a busy corner
and neither can find a thing you want
to say more than anything else right now
and so you say goodbye.

     You are not
inconsolable. You know how it feels
to go out of people's lives and
not come back. Sometimes it is
deliberate. Usually though
it is this same daily passing of things
(our minds always on what we
are about to receive). And of course
there are always others, walking in
and out of your life, but now
you notice it a little more, you begin
shaking hands, even with friends,
hugging, touching, lingering in doorways
talking about nothing much, anything,
not wanting to say goodbye just yet.

For the Woman in the Headlines

1

First steps are
    most momentous.
        Before you know

you're in the game
    your choices
        have begun to desert you.

Your birth was hardly a waking
    you thought luck
        was your birthright

your dreams
    a promised future.
        For a while too

nature
    overawed by your beauty
        hung fire.

One moment, so splendid
    you made time one
        dazzling sea

where steps you've taken
    are washed away
        into ones you might have

will take
    in one of your futures.
        But afterward this

is what you are left with:

footsteps in stone
    scars over both eyes

the keys to a home
    you never wanted
      to leave.

2

When she was found she held a few strands of hair, not her own,
wrapped round the fingers of one hand, so tight they cut the skin.

Her nose was bent, front teeth caved in like her high-heeled shoes.
Her throat had bright red bruises outlined in white.

When asked if she was ready to press charges, she declined.

3

Did he talk of love?
    Did he blind you
      in the sun of his gaze?

Did he talk of love
    when he called you
      an angel

and you gave yourself to him
    though his kisses
      tasted of smoke?

Bluebeard

He will damn himself when
he sees what he did to you
He will tear at himself
but his arms are too solid
He will throw himself at a wall
but he doesn't break
the easy way you did
His mouth is full of teeth
and curses
He calls himself worse names
than even you have called him
But he won't let you go
till you have heard them all
He will find out your number
He won't let go till he shows you
what you knew from the start
what you came to him knowing
what you saw when you looked in his eyes
the first time and couldn't turn away
He will find out your number
He'll say he wasn't himself
He will tell you everything
is different now   But
you know   have known   have not
learned from knowing
nothing changes
And when he has finished
damning himself
he will blame it on you

Diaspora

They are pictured as migrating birds of prey. But a lot of them still live in Germany. You can see their retired backsides as they bend over digging bone ash into their gardens.

In Australia too this sight occasionally mars a Sunday hike through the suburbs. And in Austria, it goes without saying, they even turn their faces to the cameras.

You see them go by all the time when you're hitchhiking from Chicago to L.A. They raise colorful scented wisteria and magnolia as far north as Barrhead, Alberta, Bergen and Göteberg.

Some still bask on the beach near Rio. Others own islands in the blue Aegean. It's hard to explore for the headwaters of the Nile without bumping into at least one or two toting cameras.

Some write books and send them round the globe in plain brown wrappers. A few sell arms to Arabs and, some say, even to Israel. One is known to have entered the Soviet Union using his own passport. The fate of others in the Eastern Bloc is obscure.

In England, though, some collect pensions and a few have gone on to head government departments. In a village of Central France, one stood for the office of mayor and won by acclamation.

Don't think they haven't suffered, though, since their Jerusalem burned. Hardly a day goes by when they don't lapse into embarrassed silence in the midst of conversation. And once in a while one begins to look for something — a silver cigarette case or other such trifle he once held dear as life — and recalls with regret that, long ago, he had to leave it behind.

In These Unspeakable Times

David, your garden opera sings
of birds and flowers — a lullaby of

what the birds witnessed
from their branches

how the flowers were
crushed by the falling body

Step out into the night and the world
screams at you

Eden! you answer
Eldorado!

Debris of the past
filters down on us all

odes to joy
empire   revolution

hot words   stockpiled in
magazines ready for firing

Memory   lethal memory
with a half-life of a thousand years